MENTAL ILLNESS REVEALED

DISTORTED MIND

Michael Fortnam

outskirtspress
DENVER, COLORADO

Outskirts Press, Inc.
http://www.outskirtspress.com

ISBN: 978-1-4787-1909-0

Outskirts Press and the "OP" logo are trademarks belonging to Outskirts Press, Inc.

PRINTED IN THE UNITED STATES OF AMERICA

For my mother,
and in the memory of my father.
They always believed in me.

TABLE OF CONTENTS

PREFACE

When I chose the title for my book to be *Distorted Mind*, I was concerned that it could convey negative connotations to some people. Certainly this is not intended.

The word distorted seemed to best describe my state of mind during my most troubled years. Unreal and sometimes multiple messages entered my thoughts. I was delusional, confused, and full of bizarre ideas. My judgment was often far removed from reality. I struggled to decipher messages that randomly occurred in my brain. Part of my mind was based in reality while at times my thoughts conflicted and were truly distorted.

In my writing I sought to describe and express what I was thinking and feeling so that others with a mental illness may realize that they are not alone in their plight. Also, I hope to help inform people about some of the facets of a mental illness.

I kept my story short, trying to stay focused on what I felt to be most important to write and most interesting to read.

INTRODUCTION

At barely twenty years old, it seemed that my life was already in total disarray. My first two years at college ended up in failure and with a great deal of uncertainty as to who I was and what I wanted to become. The long-held belief in my ability to succeed was put into doubt.

As a youth I had always believed in the strength of my mind. I thought it was safe from harm. I never considered that a sickness could occur in my thoughts. Regardless of what I may have believed, the truth was inescapable. My reasoning had become seriously disoriented and distracted from real life.

It was a couple years after high school, mixed in with the stresses of college, when I first heard what seemed like a voice inside of my head. At first it sounded like my own voice talking to me amongst my thoughts. It seemed natural at the time. I thought it was my subconscious mind at work, helping me to think and to make decisions about my life.

Gradually the bewilderment expanded. I felt as though other people had access to my mind. As time passed, the illness grew. It intruded on my sanity. I began to rely on the inner voices more and more.

When it was suggested that I see a professional for help, I resisted the idea at first. I didn't realize that I needed help, but soon consented to go to a local mental health center.

Soon I was put on anti-psychotic medication. It was so powerfully sedating that I could hardly walk. I knew that I couldn't stay on the medication. At the time I compared the oppressive feeling to wearing a chemical straitjacket.

My caseworker from the Department of Mental Health suggested that I withdraw from school to take care of myself. I wouldn't do it. I wanted to get on with my life. I had long sought the college experience, so I wasn't ready to give up on my perception of what life should be. I had the impression that fun, friends, and success would be automatic once I got to college.

My freedom to live my life with joy and hope diminished as my abilities shrank. My only rescue was the world I created in my thoughts.

I could find some solitude riding the subways to and from college. There were times when I tried to study on the train, but often I just observed my surroundings or listened to music. It fatigued me, but I took a melancholy kind of pleasure in the long commute. I liked noticing people and reading the advertisements along the subway walls. From inside the trains and buses, I quietly gazed out the windows as the scenery of life passed by.

By the time I got home I was so tired that I usually just rested and wondered what I was doing wrong that made my life so disappointing. I wanted to be able to make friends, but somehow I rarely did. There were periods when I was barely able to pass through life with all its misery.

Feelings that life was failing me began to permeate. I didn't know there was a deeper problem than just being socially unconnected. The elusive nature of my illness remained unseen to me, but it was expanding and replacing more of my common sense as time wore on. Unreal stories about who I was began to develop and occupy more of my personality.

My imagination had offered me an escape from a world that I did not seem to understand. Irrational thoughts and delusions paralleled my normal functioning. Problems distinguishing real life from my imagination were surfacing at work, home, and school.

Part of the outcome of my dilemma was that I spent a great deal of time alone, with an increasingly distorted view on reality. My loneliness evolved into isolation and despair. These feelings overwhelmed me as they crept further into my mind and state of being.

Periods of paranoia and suspicion entered my brain. I was making assumptions that had no basis in reality. Wild dreams of awe and chaos kept me at a distance from the sane world. Decisions that I made about my life were occasionally done with the guidance of what I thought was a telepathic ability. Occasionally I followed an impulse of my inner thoughts that seemed to lead me to do unusual things.

Somehow I believed I was involved in a great battle between good and evil. My perplexed mind manufactured a deep, elaborate, and complex belief system. I surmised that an evil and controlling power had put me under a drug-induced hypnosis. I felt as though my mind had been extracted and then used to produce movies and songs. My paranoia convinced me that there was a way of transferring mental and emotional reflexes of the brain onto film and audio recordings.

When I saw mental health professionals, they would ask me if I heard voices. The question troubled me, because even though I didn't feel as though I actually heard voices, I did have intrusive thoughts. They weren't exactly voices, so I wondered if this was the problem they were questioning for. I tried to explain that there were sometimes mysterious and somewhat random thoughts floating around in the back of my mind.

Expanding mental excursions occupied great lengths of time and energy. My confusions grew deeper and deeper as well as more widespread, occupying greater aspects of my life. My sense of identity was scattered. Mental exhaustion plagued me. Trying to maintain a sense of normalcy became more difficult as symptoms persisted.

Though I received help from doctors and social workers, the idea of an illness in my mind was complicated to try to understand. I didn't know what questions to ask to clarify the nonsensical parts of my thinking. Accepting their words was difficult when they tried to explain my condition to me.

It would prove to be a tremendous challenge to comprehend and appreciate the fact that many of the thoughts that determined how I saw myself were unreal!

I know the condition may be described as a chemical imbalance. For myself, and I'm sure for others who have suffered depression and other illnesses of the mind, that does not begin to describe our world! It doesn't provide one word as to what it feels like or what life problems arise. Having a mental illness is complicated, confusing, and socially difficult to live with.

A TERRIBLE ILLNESS

DEPRESSION

The paralysis of depression encompassed my very core. Its silent brutality lay hidden from view, but its power and pain struck at the will to live. It is so difficult to describe, both now years into recovery, and also while in the depths of its curse. It was grief, sorrow, regret, hopelessness, and despair. It was indescribable in so many ways. The pain was a living horror. There was a complete absence of normal feelings.

There were feelings like dread and torment. My future and my past became nothing but waste and a hopeless loss.

I felt it was as though every person in my life had died. There was no one to touch or to reach out to. It seemed as though no one could come into my life even if they knew I was dying in some awful way. My life was not happening, beyond mere existence.

What little there was of me was breaking off and sinking into nothingness. Memories of being somebody or thoughts of becoming somebody were replaced by feelings of failure and unidentifiable pain. The depression had ripped away all memory of happiness and experiences of a lifetime. Nothing was left but a dying mind full of only distortion and a bleak void.

It was as though my mind were hunting for a thought or a feeling other than grief. I think I was looking for an identity. My thoughts were seeking something to hold on to. They searched for a memory, an experience, or an emotion that was anything but dread and loss.

I surveyed my thoughts and feelings for relief from my desolation, but could find nothing that might provide any freedom from the dreadful sorrow. I continually questioned what I would have to do to be rid of the overwhelming pain. It covered me like a burdensome cloak that I could not see beyond.

I needed something to believe in. I needed something to hold on to. If I could find something good about myself, I thought that maybe there was a possibility that life could change.

I thought that if only I had friends, they could help me change my life. Maybe they could show me something good about myself, but I knew no one. This realization added to the feeling of hopeless isolation.

I needed an answer to explain the horrible pain I was in. I imagined all kinds of possibilities. Was there such a thing as God's will?

Would alcohol help alleviate the suffering? Would it provide me with a freedom of expression that I struggled to display in my daily life?

I wondered if perhaps I had denied my life's purpose and now the unused aspects were dying inside of me. Had I failed at my life? Was it regret that I was suffering from? Could I escape or remedy the loss I was feeling if I found an answer? Had I missed my opportunity to live, and was it now too late? What was happening to me, and how could the anguish stop? Everything about me seemed to be dying of an emotional cancer.

Some of my most despairing memories were in trying to find something to believe in. Finding emptiness instead left me with questions. What was life for? Why was I alone? I found no memory or feelings of worth, so therefore I had no sense of self. There was not even a remote thought or inclination to believe that I was successful at being alive.

Somehow my brain must have thought my soul was gone. I wondered if life had left me. Some kind of death had occurred.

Perhaps physically there were sections in my brain that were no longer functioning. Maybe the doctors that talked of chemical imbalance were right. It could be thought of that way, in part. A partially functioning brain regarding memory and emotion or some other realm could be the scientific answer.

This malfunction took a great toll. At times the toll was slow and lasting, while at other times it could be deep and punishing. It was a force unseen. It was an invisible power crushing over me.

The overwhelming sense of loss and dread surrounded me. It captured all my strength and will to do anything. I was mourning a deep sense of loss, but I didn't know exactly what had died.

My distress included a dreadful sadness, but there was nothing like a death or divorce to attribute it to. There was no trauma or shock that could be assigned a possible cause. There was agony with no relief in sight. It was as though death would be better.

There was no feeling of being alive or of myself ever being different or happy again. I couldn't perceive life changing to anything more than an endless torment of grief and a conquering anguish.

The pain I felt had physical nature to it at its intense moments. I remember a particular day crumbling to the kitchen floor in agony. I crawled across the floor and pulled myself up with doorknobs. My only desire was to die or to describe the misery so that someone might be able to help. I thought life must go on, but the devastating pain was unbearable.

I could not understand why I was experiencing so much unidentifiable pain. What was wrong with me? Why was I curled up on the floor? Was I being punished? Where did the pain come from? I couldn't understand.

I felt like a prisoner of brutality. That day in particular when I was lying on the floor, I recall praying that time would stop. The sun had risen and I had managed to dress for work. I was due to be at work in less than an hour. It was almost as though some supernatural power were punishing me. It was not of this world. I remember pain from all around. I just could not identify where it was coming from. There was nothing I could do to stop it.

Sleep was my best defense, but the day was moving on. I had to leave the apartment. I couldn't afford to miss any more days from work.

At one point I prayed for death. I offered God, by whatever name, to take my whole life and soul. I asked Him to please end my existence so that I did not need to live.

I remember clearly saying, "Take my life, the present, my childhood, and my future life so that I do not have to live this relentless horror and burden. Remove this great murderous oppression that surrounds and completely covers my being. Whatever is in me that's alive, let it die. Remove the cruelty of pain that I am suffering."

I made the plea again and again, "Please let my life end. Please let me die. Please remove this cruelty."

A thousand tons of burdens would come upon me as soon as I would awake in the morning. Every waking moment was pain. The threshold of suffering inside of my body and mind was so intense and overbearing.

There was no place to go to be free of the oppression and sorrow. The sadness and grief were so potent that maybe words cannot describe them. There was no escape.

If words could be found to explain the agony I felt, there would be no one who would understand — or at least no one who would be able to help. The torment of those days of deep depression was truly extraordinary. I wanted there to be a reason for my depression, but I could not find it. I could not understand why there was so much pain.

For me, depression and the related illnesses of the mind were like a sickness that I could not tell anyone I was having. I didn't know what to say. At times I would ask people if I appeared depressed, but they would generally say that I looked fine. I didn't want to look fine when I felt so bad on the inside.

At times throughout the years, the depression was sometimes only mild. During these times it was much less destructive to my ability to live life, except that it kept me rather secluded and lonesome. I still knew no escape from the malady. I just assumed that my life was a lonely one with struggles.

When I did wonder why I was so alone, I didn't know what questions to ask. I didn't know which doctors to call. First of all, I didn't know what I was suffering from. Life was so dire. I hardly knew what was happening. I knew it could be bleak and desolate with little hope, but I stayed alive. I was sure things would get better, but years kept passing on with little change in my life.

My aloneness and lack of friends were troubling to me. I wanted more from life, but I didn't know how to get it. I thought things would happen automatically.

Part of the agony of depression is that it is hard to reach out to anyone and then find a person who understands. Depression is not just a vacuous turmoil. It is also not being able to convey the barrenness. Not being able to communicate prolongs the illness and suffering until collapse, or until help arrives.

Eventually medication was prescribed and the emptiness and vacancy inside started to lessen. At first any changes were barely noticeable. As the weeks wore on after beginning the anti-depressant, I noticed that though the bleakness was still there, it might be a little less than it had been weeks or days before.

While recovering from a deep depression, I realized some part of me was still alive inside. I had feelings of wanting to be connected and understood. I gained some assurances that life would get better. I remember living in the hope of a better day. Mostly I wanted to live without the pain.

There were moments in the day as the medication began to take effect when distractions could temporarily remove me from the desolation and aloneness. A pleasant song on the car radio could bring reprieve. My imagination could take over briefly and I could get lost in the music. The sadness and despair would soon return after the song was over. Something dreadful would occupy my thoughts again. I would wait for another diversion, or search my thoughts for some sign of hope.

My family was very supportive and helpful. I could sometimes accept a compliment that I looked good or was doing well. I could return a good word with a smile, but deep inside there was still a great emptiness that no one could seem to fill. I thanked God that with the help of my family, I found help. Recovering from mental illness with prolonged depression is not only about the relief that medication provides. It also requires a continued effort to fill in the vacancies of life. The past has to be assimilated and a future needs to be found.

MANIC BEWILDERMENT

Very much opposite to depression, I also experienced serious manic episodes over the years. Feelings during a manic phase can be very exciting. There were times when I couldn't even remember what depression felt like. For starters, I loved to simply wake up in the morning. I can think of two periods, probably a spring and a summer, when I was experiencing mania. I loved being alive. I felt successful at just being me. There was an excitement to life and a lure to living. It was like a high that didn't go away.

For me the enthusiasm was a feeling dominated by creative desires and energy. I recall feelings of freedom and exuberance. There were no problems to contend with. Nothing mattered but simple enjoyments and a wide-open, wondrous future. I felt energetic and I needed to express myself by doing things creative.

What I did most of all was to spend money. I acquired musical instruments to play with and a variety of tools and objects to experiment with. I bought scientific books and antiques. I thought their lessons and meaning would be mysteriously revealed to me. I loved my photography and art. I thought I had become a scientist, an artist, a collector, and more. I believed that I had found religion.

I felt an inspiration that I didn't know how to focus. The simplest things could take on spiritual significance. I always wanted to enhance the spiritual aspects of discovery and thought. I wanted to reach greater heights of freedom, expression, knowledge, and faith. I wanted to know God. I wanted the feelings to be stronger.

Even more than the feeling I wanted proof that my art and inventive ideas were genuine. I wanted to be discovered. The manic periods were intoxicating but I wanted validation and proof for those feelings.

So much of what I had done never took into account as to how much I was spending. My entire life savings was disappearing and my credit card balances grew immensely.

When the frenzy wore off I had an empty bank account and a room full of art supplies, tools, cooking utensils and other various purchases.

Not until the phase was over would I see that something had gone wrong. My mind and thought processes were truly playing tricks on me. They were not functioning with normalcy or any sense of judgment.

Feeling spiritually divine or at least spiritually gifted was a big part of my illness. I thought my actions and beliefs would cause events to happen in other people's lives. When I would paint I thought I was painting profound works. With my camera I thought I was recording events from a time in history that would be enlightening to view. I was sure that I was going to be famous.

My mind lived in a dream of mystery and the occasional far-reaching belief of supernatural capabilities. How these dreams and fantasies began or ever came to an end, I never knew. I loved to believe what my mental state and feelings were telling me. I felt gifted, though I received no notice of my greatness.

In my craze, my knowledge seemed to expand. I thought it would go on forever. Hopes and aspirations of discovery filled my dreams. Idealizations that my life was changing in triumph filled me with false glory. I felt like a prodigy of the arts and sciences. I felt attached to God. I even believed I could speak in new parables.

Looking back, I wonder what drove the energy and bizarre behavior. It all seemed to be an attempt at breaking out of my restrictive personality. I wanted to be someone exciting. I struggled to know who I was. I tried on different roles. I would get ideas of who I might be, but then they would fade. I think I tried to define my personality with spending.

It amazed me as to what my high spirits had done when I saw the actions from the distance of time. Some part of my mind had a free will of its own, until something like running out of money would force it to stop. The joys would later seem so unreal and costly. I was not an artist and I was not an inventor. I had no spiritual awakenings.

On occasion, I felt great grandeur. I had one experience — a hallucination, some might call it — that was so profound I believed I had witnessed a vision of heaven. A great power overcame my body and I collapsed to the floor. I saw clouds open up in the sky even though I was inside my apartment. I saw the horizon in the heavens beyond the sun. It felt as though a colorless light entered my body. I thought that God was speaking to me into my subconscious. It was silent, but I craved to know what was being said to my inner mind.

Believing my mental excursions were acts of creativity or religious insights caused life changes. That strange and bizarre world in which I lived was terribly consuming. Periodically I thought to myself about being at the edge of genius. Unfortunately my inner mind did not always function in reality.

Many of the beliefs persisted after the manic phase wore off. Large segments of my life have been spent in unreal beliefs and irrational pursuits. I have always hoped not to lose all of my creative flow, but many of my previous hard-held beliefs and false insights into life had to be let go of somehow. I dearly wanted to believe all was not lost from the delusional periods of my life. There were happy times, but they weren't grounded in reality — and sadly, I was still very much alone.

EMPTY and INTRUSIVE THOUGHTS

My sense of self was so vacant and void of feelings other than loss and sorrow that I hardly knew what life was for. I didn't know what it was supposed to be, if anything at all. I didn't know what was wrong, so I guess that I took my lot in life pretty much as it came. It seemed to come without instructions.

Finding neither success nor outright failure, I struggled and pondered aimlessly throughout much of my life without experiencing its value or happiness. I looked around and found only reminders of lost opportunities. Past possibilities that never materialized plagued me.

With a complicated collection of bizarre thoughts occupying my mind, I spent many years hidden from real life.

I didn't know how to involve myself with others. I was not comfortable or happy within myself as I endured the distress of life.

For years I wondered if other people's lives were built around isolation and an absence of self-esteem as mine was. Time passed as I waited, half expecting to be found or discovered somehow.

The incompleteness I felt came from deep in the marrow of my being. It became so immensely overpowering that I felt crippled by despair. I merely suffered through my life by the wayside, not knowing how to become alive and free.

The separation I felt was as though life played on without me. I was in the audience while the world proceeded all around me. Desperately I wanted to touch it and to be part of it, but I didn't know how.

I lived for so many years in depression that I felt that I barely existed at all. Functioning somewhere between feelings of abandonment and oppression was the essence of my life. I felt as though society had found me guilty of some sort of a crime. It seemed that I was a failure to the world and to myself. I anticipated rejection and I was sure that I would simply be lost or discarded by life.

The best I could do was to grab a cup of coffee and sit down and watch. My favorite place was South Station in Boston, where I could almost feel myself as a member of the anonymous crowd passing through or waiting for trains to arrive and to depart.

Unseen to all but a few and noticed perhaps by none, I was left alone. Feeling unapproachable and unobserved,

I continued on with my life. I simply disappeared into the midst of my delusions. So much of my life had been spent looking out into a world in which I felt that I never belonged.

Sometimes hope would blink on and off. Other times, I just seemed to close my eyes and walk ahead into an uninviting future. I didn't seem to fear the future in any profound way. It was just that I saw nothing worth living for.

Everything I thought or did seemed to lead nowhere. I found only closed doors, dead ends, and despair. As I struggled along, with the passing of time I learned to cope. Wherever I went, there would be nothing there when I arrived. I could see no rewards for the process of life. I had spent all of my years trying so hard to do what was right.

Instead of developing my emotions and social skills to involve myself in the joys of life, I had my delusions. Socially I couldn't connect. I wondered what I was doing wrong. I didn't know if I was at fault.

My life seemed to travel on a different path than my peers' lives. At times my only relief was just to know that there was pain out there in other people's lives besides my own. Many of my days were painfully spent alone in my room or apartment, trying to understand my absence of belonging. My lack of friendships left me feeling unusual and different. I functioned, but life was quite barren.

For me life tended to be divided into two worlds. Outwardly my appearance would generally seem relatively normal most of the time. Unseen to most was also an inner self that was full of delusion, confusion, and loss. Living in some sort of invisible enclosure caused problems. Great conflicts emerged, which created anxiety and distress with my employment and other daily activities. It was difficult trying to manage my life in the real world.

Did my confusions and collection of irrational thoughts exist in other people's lives? What had my mind made up, and what was true? I didn't always know the difference.

Many happenings and situations alive in my mind had never really occurred at all. I had to wrestle with evidence versus doubt and delusion as I tried to decide which ones were true. My brain would deliver me unclear messages, and I would try to interpret them with my strangely abstract reasoning.

I would pass the time in months and years, hoping something would change. Sometimes I hardly noticed the years go by, yet other times I suffered terribly and was tormented by my sense of abandonment and the anguish of depression.

Imagined fears of perceived threats from people occupied my mind and affected my behavior. I often feared my bosses, the police, and most authority figures. A great deal of my time was spent in a disturbed sense of paranoia. Trying to make sense of what would prove to be irrational thoughts was exhausting. At times, my mind would instruct me to do bizarre and unusual things. I felt that I was being watched, followed, and recorded by some unknown source.

I tried to use this imaginary surveillance to deliver messages to the outside world. I remember sitting in my car and walking in the woods, telling stories out loud, thinking that I was being observed. In this way I thought that my thoughts were getting out into the public knowledge. At times I believed that I was a secret government agent, while at other times I thought I was an entrepreneur, artist, or inventor.

Other times I think I simply disappeared inside my mind for the innocent amusement of it, and to feel momentarily uplifted and fulfilled. I would conjure up new and imaginary lives to believe in, and adventures to dream.

Reading social cues correctly has always been a source of discomfort and even confusion. As a result of having little experience interacting with people, my responses could be peculiar or simply absent.

My lack of confidence made me feel weak. I didn't know what to believe, so I learned to rely on other people's opinions. Articulating myself was like reaching into an empty pool. Trying to express likes, dislikes, wants, wishes, and opinions always left me feeling as though I didn't know what to say.

My thoughts were so full of abstract analysis that I seldom if ever felt comfortable just being me. I simply couldn't understand what I was supposed to do. I often wondered where the rules came from and who decides what is right. Whose opinion counts?

Making decisions was difficult, and a daily challenge. So often I was unsure as to what was real. Perspective on real-life goals and aspirations, as well as expectations, was obscure at best.

In truth, I craved to be understood and accepted. I wanted to reach out to others to know if anyone felt as I did. I wanted to know if they were plagued by distress and uncertainty about life.

The difficulty was in communicating that I was alive and willing to belong. I yearned for the unknown people that would pass through my life to know how I felt. I wanted them to know that I was alive on the inside, but that I was having trouble getting myself out in the open. I longed for the people I hadn't met to find me.

I enjoyed the solitude of life sometimes, but other times I dearly wanted to know what else there was to do in life. Quietly I wondered what the majority of people experienced in their lives that made them feel complete.

ARREST

DISASTER

There were many years when fantasies about life filtered through my mind while I put on an appearance of normalcy. The stories in my head escalated and became more spectacular to believe.

I think I needed to believe that my life was much more adventurous and exciting than it really was. Somehow I wanted to be great so I would let myself believe in the unreal pictures floating amongst my thoughts. I allowed this creativity to occupy more and more of my time and thoughts as the days, months, and years passed on. Eventually all of the confusion and unrealities, which I believed at least in part to be true, would be forced into conflict with reality.

I found out the hard way that I needed more help. I was seeing a psychiatrist on a fairly regular basis, but I wasn't being entirely forthright about the inner workings of my thoughts. I had a couple of years of modest freedom from depression, but something else was lurking in the recesses of my mind. I was not at rest. I didn't realize that I was still sick in yet another way.

I had become confused and unsure about life. My speculations as to its purpose and my belonging did not always seem to come true. I was fraught with doubts about my beliefs and I wanted them clarified and rectified. I wanted proof that my beliefs were real. I didn't know what I could believe in, and I knew that I was beginning to fray. Meaningless bliss intermingled with irrational fears were the building blocks of my existence.

I hadn't developed any lasting friendships. There was nothing to vary my life from working in the daytime hours and sleeping at night. Leading up to my fall from that lonely place, I began to drive excessively. I would get in my car and drive for the excitement and action of being behind the wheel. I enjoyed an aggressive sense of authority and power from driving. It also gave me a feeling of comfort and energy.

I would leave work in the early evening and then make a network out of stopping off at coffee shops later in the evenings after work. Sometimes I would spend hours driving before I went home to my apartment. On weekends especially I remember that I would play favorite motivational music to make the drive more exciting. Many times I felt like I was going out on a mission. In fact, in a way that was the purpose behind my thrill drives.

Somewhere around this time, my office personality and behavior were beginning to change. They were beginning to take on more of the role of my nighttime personality. The quiet disturbances in my thoughts were becoming more dominant. The belief that I had special powers was getting stronger.

My nighttime fantasies and delusions started to occupy more and more of my daytime hours. It became so that work began to interfere with my evenings, rather than my evenings being an escape from work. I was adding hundreds if not thousands of miles to my car without going anywhere in particular. I just drove to familiar parts of the city and towns, searching for new coffee shops where I could stop off. They were like checkmarks on the imaginary map I kept in my head.

I began to interpret meaning in people and in things that I saw. I felt that I could interpret meaning from a building's architecture or a person's clothing. Countless objects and events, and people's actions, began to take on more and more complex and multiple meanings in my head.

I was getting superstitious and paranoid. To make matters still more complex was the fact that my psychiatrist was involved in my paranoia. In my mind he was one of the players in an elaborate imaginary life that I had been creating in my irrational mind.

My personality at work may have been tending toward the antagonistic, but it's hard to really know. I was including my bosses and coworkers in my unreal life that my illness had created deep inside my thoughts. The difficulty was that they were becoming in some part obstacles to my new outlook on reality.

Just to make things a little worse, I think I had become a bit careless about taking the medications that I was on. I was suffering an illness in my mind, but had no comprehension of the deception it created. My thoughts had become a maze of conflict, and it was affecting my decisions, activities, and behaviors.

This brings me to the turning point in my illness and my life. I chose a day when I was determined to know the truth. I decided to challenge my thoughts with my actions. It would be a reality test with risk! It evolved into a life-changing episode.

I put the ambiguities and fears that perplexed my thoughts to the test in my apartment one day. The result was a disaster! My career, that I had such a tremendously difficult time trying to get started, would be crushed. My decision to conduct a reality test ended up creating a new bottom of despair and grief in my already beleaguered life.

My confused actions and inner disharmony had conflicted with the real world before. This time my mental illness would involve the police. No longer would my mind be free to ponder the circumstances of my life. My sense of grand omnipotence and divine thoughts would receive a shock into reality.

My eventual collapse began when I started making a little too much noise pretending to be having an argument with an imaginary girlfriend in my apartment. In fact, there was no one in the apartment but me. I started banging a pan on the counter and yelling something loudly across the room, as though someone were there.

The noise was enough for a neighbor to call the police. The police met me in the stairwell as I walked down from the third floor.

Later I would learn the police report said I had powder in my hair. It turns out it was baby powder. Before I left the apartment, I had squirted baby powder at the ceiling lamp in the kitchen. I was convinced that there might be a camera in the light spying on me. That morning I had concluded that the reason the landlord had changed the lamp fixture was not energy conservation, but to install a hidden camera. I thought the baby powder would obscure the camera's view.

At first the police let me go. I told them I hadn't heard anything. Just as I was about to leave in my car, they stopped me in the parking lot. They asked me to return inside. They wanted to go into my apartment to be sure everything was okay. I let them in.

The place was strewn from one end to the other with clutter. My art projects and would- be inventions and all the things I had purchased were essentially dumped everywhere. There was baby powder strewn all over the place.

One of the police officers saw something that I had made. It drew alarm from her and she told me not to touch it. It was a pipe about fourteen inches long with a cap-bolt on each end. She would later write it up in the police report as a suspected pipe bomb. It was nothing more than a small piece of pipe that I liked the look and feel of. I said it was a piece of art. I really didn't know what I had made it for. In some way I thought it did have some sort of spiritual power. I thought it was symbolic.

They let me go and I went to work. Within a couple of hours, the police called me at work and asked me to return to my apartment. I sent an e-mail to my manager and left the building. Little did I know that I would never return.

When I returned to my apartment that day, I was shocked. I had taken my time getting back to the apartment. I had stopped off for a cup of coffee and probably had it in my hand as I drove up. There were a fire truck and two police cruisers waiting there! There were a couple of other cars there also. I saw someone who looked like a reporter taking notes, but thankfully I didn't see any camera trucks.

I parked in the handicapped spot as instructed and got out. They told me to sign a piece of paper that would allow them into my apartment. Even though the police officer had just told me that they were already looking around in my apartment, I still signed, to be cooperative. One man talked to me and said he was from some special services or some division chief, and I heard what sounded like "bomb squad." Astonished, I wondered what was going on.

Soon a man with gloves on came out of the apartment building carrying something. I didn't like the look on his face. The two men talked briefly and looked at what he had brought out. It was a little glass jar with an ounce or so of kerosene and a handkerchief in it. They told me to smell it and ask me what I thought it was. They were going to take it to the lab to identify its contents, but it was enough to make an arrest. They said it was an explosive device.

I had to pay for my mental excursion. When I put the object together some days before I thought I was being instructed by God to create a formula that would lead to a cure for cancer. It had stuff like salt, sugar, baking soda, and maybe even a little yeast in the mixture. It was evidence to the police — and it was what they thought it was, not what I thought it was, that mattered! This seemed to be the crux of matter as far as my state of being was concerned! What my mind had previously been telling me did not agree with society's view, and I was on the losing end of the objections.

After the police searched my apartment on this terrible day, my previous life ended. I was put under arrest and taken into custody. I didn't understand why! In a complete state of shock, I wondered what I had done. I immediately pledged to cooperate, out of fear. I was sure there was a misunderstanding or some kind of terrible mistake. Someone's observations and judgment were very much amiss, I was sure. I couldn't believe what was happening.

I looked at the sky over my apartment as they put me in handcuffs behind my back. The police, I now realized, were deadly serious. I said my silent prayer to who I felt to be God in Heaven. I put my full faith and trust in Him as my mind steered me toward desperate faith.

It was time to discover if I was a divinely inspired servant of God, or if there was the possibility that my brain was malfunctioning and telling me lies. I stood firm and erect, believing that surely this was my test of faith. My reality test was becoming powerfully real.

I knew my inner faith would be challenged, and this was it. I had to believe that this was my course in life. I had to believe it was laid out for me to experience and to follow. It would shape me and I would serve God, I prayed. I desperately hoped that there would be nothing that I couldn't handle, and that it was God's will that I had to accept, no matter were it led.

I had taken silent vows of simplicity and poverty if it was in His will during the solitude of my days and evening over the proceeding months. I had a belief that I had been communicating with God at some level for some time, months, maybe years prior to this episode. I was willing to use my strengths and goodness for the benefit of addressing the needs of society. I felt that if I were put into a situation of despairing need, that I would be able to find and thus map out a way of survival and eventual happiness for others and myself.

My pleading hope was that this new direction of my life, which had now irrevocably begun, was a new beginning. I was silent but desperate. Was I being saved, or was I totally wrong, and thus my life lay in ruin?

I was ripped from my old life as a seemingly rather ordinary person going about his day to a suspect in jail. A new reality was forced upon me with certainty, and there was no way to retreat.

I was no longer in charge of my own choices or my mental state. I couldn't go or do what I wanted anymore. My erratic travels were now suddenly stopped. There was nowhere for me to go to now. I could not change my world by changing my thoughts anymore, because my freedoms had been taken away.

My thoughts as to what was supposed to happen didn't come true. There was nowhere to turn. I was put under arrest, and my opinions and wishes didn't count anymore.

My mental pleasures and imagination were rapidly becoming whitewashed into a nearly forgotten realm. The life I had been accustomed to was being stripped away.

The police took charge of my life. They would now decide whether my actions were acceptable or not. They were not interested in my thoughts. They searched only for evidence and facts and witnesses to my behavior. What I thought was true or what I thought I was doing no longer mattered. I was no longer in control of my life. My freedom was gone.

At the police station, I called my parents to tell them that I was in trouble. The police said I had an explosive device — an "inferno machine," they called it. I was distraught. My parents said that they would be right there. It was about an hour's drive. I remember getting my mug shot taken, front and side. I must have been fingerprinted. Being processed as a criminal scared me and left me dazed. My whole body must have been shaking. I couldn't comprehend what was happening to me. My weekend was spent curled up on the floor of a jail cell under the bench. My mind raced in silent terror as I waited, not knowing what was to happen next.

On the following Monday I was taken to court. Through a family connection, I received the best public defender they had. I got assurances that I wasn't the typical type of person who came through the jail. My lawyer assured me that things would work out okay. Her immediate objective was to keep me out of prison and get me a mental health evaluation.

LOCKED WARD

Handcuffed to my seat Monday evening after court, I was taken away in a sheriff's van. There was a heavy protective screen between me and the other suspects that divided us from the driver and his partner. One man sat next to me and there were two women in back. I couldn't see them, but I heard their voices and screams.

I don't clearly remember the whole trip from the courthouse, but I know we stopped to drop off the women at their prison first.

Next we went to a high-security prison for men. We drove into a garage and the van was inspected. I was unloaded and was told to sit on a bench. I was frightened that a mistake had been made. When I left the court it was my understanding that I was to be sent to a psychiatric hospital for evaluation.

The guards patted me down again and had me take off my shoes so that they could inspect them. I felt as though they were laughing at me. I must have looked dazed and confused, because I surely was. I was terrified at the thought of spending even one night in prison.

I heard screams of men from beyond the wall, where I couldn't see. The guards and employees out front were not fazed.

I waited without a word or a movement for what felt like hours. Maybe I was just being processed on through to my final destination, I thought.

While I waited at the prison, I was put in an enclosed room made of Plexiglas walls, with some other men.

We were offered trays of food to eat. Most of the others stood back and rejected it. It was as though the whole process was second nature and very familiar to them. They seemed to be watching me with amusement when I tried something to eat. I thought, why not? It could help calm my nerves. I didn't know what they were laughing about, so I put the food back and tucked myself up against the wall for a sense of security.

Suddenly a fight broke out. I thought a younger man of about twenty or so was coming after me, but he viciously attached another older man. He punched his face until a guard came in and broke it up. The guard told the fighter, "Now you're going upstate!" I couldn't imagine what awaited him.

Greatly relieved and in a delirious state of shock, I was eventually returned to the van and we drove away. This time it was just the two guards and me. I had no idea what awaited me.

Soon we arrived at my destination. A doctor examined me before I was admitted.

My memory is blurry, but I remember passing out when the nurse took a blood sample from my arm. The feeling of my blood being drawn from my body, with a heightened sensitivity, made me faint and weak. I went into a blackout. I woke up on the floor of the quiet room with a large woman holding a small brown paper bag over my mouth to help me relax my breathing. She spoke to me in a non-threatening manner to calm my nerves.

All of the walls were padded and on the floor was a thick rubbery mat. There was a small viewing window in the door, but I couldn't stand up to see out of it.

When the nurse left me alone, I lay on the floor motionless, listening for the slightest sound. I didn't know if my life was over. I could hear faint voices outside the door as I trembled, not knowing who might come in and what would happen next. Fear eventually gave way to sleep.

When I woke and listened to the voices in the hall, I heard that they had a hard time finding an available bed.

Soon I was taken to a conference room where they had a roll-up bed. This was to be my room for the night. Sleep was difficult and frightful. I was uncomfortable and dazed, plus the room was hot.

Every noise and footstep sent a shock through my nerves. The next morning a nurse awakened me. I found myself unharmed after my first night. In the slightest degree I felt a mild sense that I might be okay for the time being.

I soon realized that I had in fact been involuntarily admitted to a state psychiatric hospital. It was the initial phase of my sentence. My public defender had kept me out of prison — at least for the time being.

I would still have to be evaluated for competency to stand trial and culpability at the time of the alleged crime, so I wasn't out of the woods yet. I was hardly aware of what the legal terms meant.

At that stage, still in my delirious and shocked state of mind, I didn't realize that I would have to return to court after psychiatric recommendations were made. It was still necessary for me to be interviewed by a court-appointed specialist. She would make her recommendation to the court as to my mental state.

In the beginning I tried to stay safe as I adjusted to my new surroundings. We were provided information on hepatitis and HIV/AIDS, which didn't help ease my concerns regarding my new environment. I didn't want to think about the danger I was in. I didn't know the safety of the hospital.

After meeting with a psychiatrist, I would soon be medicated and feel semi-comatose from side effects.

The first decision of the court was that I would spend the next twenty days in the state psychiatric hospital to be reviewed and assessed. When I returned to court, the twenty-day review and observation was increased to forty days for continued observation and evaluation of the effects of the medications they were prescribing me.

Observations were documented from everyone on the ward, whether I had any contact with them or not. There were doctors, nurses, social workers, interns, and advocates throughout the hospital on any given day.

My hospital stay would be greatly extended as my life took on its new course. During my stay, I surrendered to the certainty that there are no promises in life. Previous to my arrest, I was sure that everything good and grand that I imagined myself to be would eventually be revealed.

Dramatically, that Friday morning's reality test proved everything was going the other way. My perceptions of life and reality were not in agreement with what life really is.

Somehow I thought the relative ease of staying out of harm's way was automatic. I didn't know how abruptly life could change! I thought a person had to look for trouble to find it. Maybe that is what I did. I didn't know it could be thrust upon a person as suddenly as it had happened to me.

Somehow I never realized that a mental illness could bring upon such sharp changes to life. It could happen to anyone, no matter who they were — because it was happening to me. I held on to some obscure hope that it could be a test of faith. The thought that I was sick and my life was shattered would take time to gradually consider accepting.

At some point during my experience there, I began to uncover and unravel the misinterpretations that I had created for myself. Perceptions of the world had undergone a series of twists and deviances over time. Some adverse behaviors and memories were simple and easier to accept and change, while others — such as imagined religious insights and profound hallucinations — proved more difficult to overcome. My new understanding was devastating to my state of being and sense of self. My old consciousness gradually gave way to a new reality.

My new life was beginning to form around me. I wasn't the person I thought I was. I felt that I wasn't even average anymore. I thought that now I was mentally less stable than the normal and average person. I began to think that I was different because I had an illness. When it came upon me, I didn't know — and I of course had no idea were it would take me next.

True calamity, such as prison, had been averted thus far — but my life had fallen off its tracks. I was stunned because of what had been lost. A state of shock, and fear of the unknown held me in its grip. I didn't know the extent of my catastrophe. I didn't know how hard and deep I would fall as I lay in wait in the lonely mysterious halls of the psychiatric hospital.

The medication I was prescribed held my anxiety in check. I didn't panic. It was generally quiet, so I was deeply grateful for this stroke of good fortune. A disaster had befallen me in the prime years of my life, but it still could have been worse.

I was not in jail. I was in a hospital. The possibility of being sent to jail remained a possibility. I prayed that my bottom would remain right there where I stood. My mind was crashing all around me in the hospital's locked ward. There was no screaming, and there were no fights. I was not being threatened. In fact, I felt as though I were being cared for. I wasn't sure that I could trust the relative peace surrounding my fear of this helpless unknown. I was at the mercy of someone or something beyond my control.

All I could do was to keep my head down and stay quiet. I decided I would not talk unless spoken to. I would not hide, but I would try to blend in so as to go as unnoticed as possible. I decided to be as friendly as I could muster through my depression. I accepted the help of the staff when offered. I tried not to get angry or upset at anything. I didn't complain about the food or the room. The facilities were not to be criticized, because I knew it could be a million times worse.

After I knew I wasn't going to be sent to jail, but that I would stay at the hospital indefinitely, I breathed a sigh of relief and gratitude.

The pain of truly being nobody overwhelmed me. I slowly began to replace the self-perception that I was noble and somehow ordained by God with the idea of an illness in my mind.

There was something wrong with the way I thought and perceived life around me. My opinions were obscure at best. No one else out there saw the things that I did. My mind and thoughts lived independently of the mainstream of life. In fact, my thoughts were not always based in reality, and apparently some considered me unsafe.

What I thought was ingenuity went beyond creative impulse and entered what must seemingly be called insanity. That dreadful word apparently applied to me — at least in part.

How much of me could be insane, if that was the word for it? I always knew and felt there was proof that I was not completely insane. After all, I held a job. I drove a car. I paid bills and maintained conversations. Surely I wasn't insane. Could mental illness be a partial insanity, I wondered?

Would there be help? Would there be a cure? I had received life-saving help from my depression before. What was I facing now?

I supposed that a new life would slowly emerge if I surrendered to the inevitable truth. I wasn't in charge of my future. Were doctors in charge? Was it a judge? Was it God, on some distant plane? Who would be taking charge of my life? How much say would I have?

For now, the State Department of Mental Health would be in charge of my care and immediate future. I would do the best I could to survive the ordeal and maybe one day find value and reason.

In my mind, I didn't know how I would manage. How would I be able to determine truth from fiction? It would become necessary for my survival to learn how.

My new and great challenge was the mental struggle to separate imagination and grandiosity from reality. My new life, if I were to have one, depended upon it. I needed to learn how to live. Just as if I had a physical handicap, I needed to learn how to live again in a new way.

I knew I hadn't caused my confusions. I didn't plan on being mentally ill. In the beginning — and for a long time — I tried to pretend that I wasn't. As a matter of fact, I really didn't know what it meant.

Instead of looking for success, I found myself desperately trying to cope. How would I cope with the losses? How would I cope with the knowledge that this time I was truly mentally ill and it couldn't be hidden? What did it say about my future? Could I have one? These were some new questions I began to ask as time alleviated the immediacy of the crisis.

No one could protect me from my demise now. I couldn't pretend my illness wasn't real. Truth had been shown to me. I had never in my life imagined that I might be arrested one day. I never thought about being mentally ill aside from bouts of depression, which were severe enough on their own.

The possibility of my becoming sick beyond my depression had never occurred to me. I thought I was exempt from further mental illness. I hadn't even accepted my depression in the past, and now the doctors were diagnosing me with schizoaffective disorder. I never once considered the possibility of such a serious illness and the stigma that accompanies it. I thought I was above it, or somehow protected from these setbacks and crises.

Earlier in life, I had always been so sure of myself. I had an inner confidence that I would always be strong and that I would succeed at life.

For a long time I tried to find some gain from my arrest and the destruction of my just- developing career hopes. Learning to understand and work with my illness had to occur sometime. I had to give it more seriousness than I had in the past. I never realized to what extent problems could arise by being careless with my medication and less than forthright with my doctor.

Before my life of delusion was crushed, there were always hopes and dreams. As the days and months went on, reality forced itself upon me. I would still reach for meaning and search my emptiness for faith, but this time I needed to know if it was true. I wondered about other people and if there were some who lived with mental problems like my own.

I held on to faint hope that I would meet someone someday who was similar to me in some ways. I wanted him or her to have known confusion and the mental flights of fantasy. I wanted to share the depression and the thrill of a manic period. I wanted to tell about the brief episodes of joy, only to be followed by catastrophic and painful loss.

NEW VIEWS
ON LIFE

A SENSE
OF STIGMA

I found myself pacing the hall of the state psychiatric hospital, not quite sure why I was there. As the days wore on into weeks and months, I gradually felt less threatened by my surroundings, but some patients were still uncomfortable to be around. Some were angry, and some couldn't be understood when they spoke. Others milled about or talked with each other like old friends. I didn't know how to respond to most of them. It was a very unfamiliar environment.

Feelings that I was being assigned to a lower class started to emerge. It seemed this hidden community of people was becoming my new peers.

I was being confronted by life. The feelings were odd and uncomfortable. I was mentally ill, but even after many years of coping with it prior to this hospitalization, I still denied its reality in my life. I had now been officially labeled. I felt as though I had been demoted by society.

A transformation of my identity was becoming clear from early on. The sense that I had been reduced to a lower class permeated my stay. No one was telling me this, but the feeling came upon me just the same. I felt as though I had been or was being segregated from society.

There was a sense of "them and us," sometimes. I was being assimilated as a member of a new class. It was stigma that I was feeling. I applied it to myself.

I was bothered by some of the rules of my new surroundings. I didn't like where I was, and I didn't like my new identity. I was no longer free, and not in charge of my whereabouts. I had been arrested and was now considered mentally ill.

I was essentially an inmate. There was a door at the end of the hall that was locked securely at all times, with a security guard stationed behind a see-through enclosure.

My circumstances left me in shock and disbelief. I thought it was beneath me to have to stand in lines for meals and medications.

I passed judgment on my new status, though I hoped to escape it somehow. I didn't want to be "one of them." I had done my best to keep my mental disturbances and depression hidden from public view up to this juncture in my life. I believed that my condition had gone relatively unnoticed in the past. Perhaps this had not been true, but I thought it was.

My primary concern was getting out of the physical confinement of the hospital. I didn't want people to know I was there. I didn't want a record. Being held on the locked ward kept me nearly cut off from the world.

In my mind, distinguishing myself from the long-term

patients seemed essential to my early release. If there were a stigma to mental illness, I wanted to face it with more freedom, which lay beyond the hospital grounds. I wanted the chance to prove myself.

I would wait each week for meetings with the doctors and social workers. Their evaluations, treatments, and recommendations were determining my fate in no small way. In one respect, they were the highlight of the week. They were someone to talk to. I craved that maybe they could tell me something about my new self and my new future.

I also wanted to know what I did that was so terrible that had gotten me there in the first place. My arrest was so sudden and unexpected. My life had been shaken to the core.

At times I deeply doubted my ability to function on my own again as a clear-minded and coherent person. I dragged my fatigued body around the ward, wondering what was to become of me.

It was hard to fight off the need to sleep excessively, due to the side effects of medication and lack of constructive things to do.

I feared being trapped in the bureaucracy of the state's mental health system. Feeling so little control over my own life, I wondered how I would ever be released from their custody and care. I worried what would become of my life when I left the hospital and its supports.

The recovery team of doctors, nurses, and social workers included me in a couple of their meetings to make a plan for my recovery and eventual discharge. They wanted me to be a participant in my own care — and thus, wanted my opinions and thoughts. My sense of personal identity was elevated that they cared so much as to include me in the planning process.

The plan that was talked about by my recovery team was that I would be released to some form of supported housing arrangement. While I had high hopes of returning to work by pretending none of this was happening, my social workers were preparing for disability benefits and transitional assistance from the State.

Convinced that my mind and emotions were essentially fine and functional, I quietly and reservedly opposed the idea that I needed so much help.

After the medication had alleviated most of the pain, I thought that I was equipped to walk on my own. I didn't know the extent or depth of my illness.

My wish was to reject any thought or mention of mental illness and return to a life that disregarded its importance and significance in my life. Somehow I knew that was not going to be completely possible. Gradually I accepted that it wasn't going to just go away and to be forgotten. My identity would not be the same as it had been before my episode.

The stigma of mental illness would seem to mark my new identity. It was more than I could bear in the beginning. I didn't know what it meant or would mean to my life. People would look at me differently, I was sure. Somehow I held on to the hope that I could escape it all with continued denial. Would there be help assimilating back into society? Troubling thoughts weighed heavily upon my mind throughout my stay at the hospital and beyond. I figured people would look upon me as one of life's failures.

Fears about my life and future compounded and never seemed to end. Worries as to whether I would I ever have the possibility of a comfortable life again were relentless.

I thought my freedom to be who I wanted to be was lost. I thought my skills and capabilities were gone. I thought I was to be set back from society even more than I already was. I didn't know where it would end. I felt that the life of the homeless was only one step away.

The staff at the hospital tried to inform us patients about some of the basic truths regarding mental illness. I tried to believe what they said. I read that mental illness affects all kinds of people, regardless of their background. It could strike anyone. I was told people still lived normal and productive lives. I wanted one. I wanted one better than I had before.

Telling or not telling prospective future employers was a worry that consumed time and energy. How much would they need to know about my illness? Would it even have to come up in an interview at all? I wondered. Should I lie about the many months that I was in the hospital? Thoughts and worries persisted at great length concerning my life returning to work. Finding a job after leaving the hospital occupied my mind far more than preparing for my emotional and social well-being.

While waiting to be released from the hospital, I had hoped my acceptance of some change or adjustments to my lifestyle would be sufficient to my recovery.

The hospital staff that had charge over my care and my future discharge prepared me for supportive living. They talked about follow-up care and therapy. They talked about taking appropriate measures to avoid a relapse and a return to the hospital in the future. They wanted me to have a network of support and to be aware of my triggers, to avoid relapse.

They seemed to have checks and balances that kept everything happening slowly. For me it was depressing and discouraging to have to spend so much time secluded from a life outside of the hospital. To me these periods of waiting were greater and greater lapses of time that would have to be explained when I looked for work. The staff said it cold be years before I could be back to full-time work! I found this hard to believe, and I couldn't accept it. I didn't want aftercare. I considered how probation might interfere with my finding a nine-to-five type of job.

Toward the end of my stay, I was shuttle bussed to a work-assistance program in a nearby city. We talked about what I was interested in and what kind of work I thought I could do. I had mixed feelings during this period of early recovery.

On one hand, there was the thought of being released from the physical limitations of the hospital setting and re-entering the real world of a non-institutionalized life. On the other hand, I was considered high-functioning, but the type of work we talked about was remedial. Yet I was still intimidated by it! It was a mental dilemma that I didn't know what I could do about.

FIRST ACCEPTANCE

Before my fated fall, I was sure that life would open up before me. The deeper and more obscure aspects of my disability had been creeping into my life without my realizing it. I could see and feel my depression, but the delusional thoughts were more abstract and difficult to acknowledge.

As I came to a new awareness, I considered the possibility that I no longer had a past to rely on. I hardly dared to face my future. My mind couldn't be trusted. What I had thought were memories of greatness and superlatives were turning out to be false perceptions. I had to learn what was true and what was imaginary. Fantasy and delusion had kept me from the realities of daily life.

The foundations that had built my life, such as my education and work history, had fallen by the wayside. Discovering that my mental excursions, which took me on trips of fantasy and battles of glory, were false beliefs caused new trials for me to face.

My purpose and challenge in life had taken a dramatic turn. Now I needed to begin a frightful search for reality and a new life.

Discovering that my mind had deceived me began most seriously after my arrest. I had to re-evaluate my past and rethink my future life.

Looking forward, I didn't see many possibilities. Somehow I thought the dead ends and misgivings from my earlier days would continue.

After many months of being in the hospital, I could not stop mourning my past and peering into a bleak future. My life had become a wreck. As my new life unraveled, I couldn't see an outlook that was any different from the tired and lonely secluded life that I had already been living previously. I felt that for me to enter the real world again could only be worse after my hospitalization.

My bizarre behaviors of years past had caught up to me. Finding a positive outlook was a challenge. I felt so debilitated. I didn't know how much recovery I had in me.

I didn't know if my illness would have a cure — or at least a remedy to lessen its profound effects. My fear was that I would not even be able to get back to my previous standard of living. Having fallen so hard and so far, I didn't even know where I could begin to start anew.

Up to this point, my life had been crowded with questions, followed by excuses for my isolation. I never had wanted to be alone. It just turned out that way. There was some relief with my newfound knowledge of my dilemma. It wasn't my fault, and I didn't always have choices. Some of my shame and guilt was lessened when I slowly began my acceptance. I wondered how seriously and how far back the illness had been active in my life.

Eventually I knew that I would get beyond my immediate circumstances. My willingness to try to live helped me see past the possibility of becoming entombed in the mental heath system.

Daily I learned to recognize the likelihood that I would not be able to pick up the life I had been living previously. I had to give up the hope that I could go on as though nothing had changed. I just sincerely wanted to be able to find something to make of myself, and to have the ability to do it.

Only after a month or two in the hospital, fifteen years after my first awareness of some problem, did I ever really begin to acknowledge or try to accept that I might truly have a mental illness. The term mental illness was troubling. Getting perspective on what it meant was a daily challenge. Understanding my problems as an illness helped alleviate some of the sense of failure and guilt.

Consenting to the fact that I needed help was new for me. I wondered how much aid and assistance I would need. I could no longer deny the need for help, so I began to grant myself permission to accept it.

The illness had been treated before with therapy and medication, but I had never fully recognized it as something permanent. I had never believed in the seriousness of it before. I never knew how real it was to my life.

I strained to see the future. While still at the hospital, I had attempted to pressure the minister for answers. The minister once said something close to, "Hope can come from our struggle and hope does not fail us." I found myself holding on to what I could remember of his words.

When I needed hope, I sometimes prayed and remembered what he had said. He had also talked about life being a process. This helped me realize that answers and freedoms would not happen all at once, so I shouldn't give up. I remember he said more than once to stay in the process. I reflected on what he meant by process, or what process I might be in.

Was the process one of my own choosing, or was it one that God had set out for me? I thought about the possibility of God's will and considered how it might come about. I asked the minister directly if God did have a will. My hope was to find meaning in my troubles and hardships. I always wished to turn my hardships into gains. He said that God would always make good out of bad if you followed Him with faith. I tried to understand what he meant by this and how it might happen.

My feeling was that everything would fall into place and have reason if I could find some measure of achievement and purpose. I wanted to be free from anxiety and loss. I compared myself countless times with others and their lives.

True acceptance was still out of reach. I realized that I carried an illness in my mind. It affected my thoughts and my mood. The illness had wreaked havoc over the years. Sometimes it was more vivid, but other times its lurking presence did its damage more silently.

Finally I could admit to it and begin to manage my illness. At least I had a chance against my previously unknown enemy. The chaos that occupied so much of my mind sub-sided significantly. I didn't carry a collection of inner thoughts confusing me with bizarre questions. My focus was centered on the real world where people lived. My mind was still busy concerning itself with how my illness affected my past and where the future might lead, but at least the thoughts were sane.

A NEW OUTLOOK

A new foundation for my life began to form when I was arrested and legally found to be mentally ill. I knew my life still existed, but it seemed to be buried under a confused identity and a great deal of uncertainty. Bringing it to the surface would take time.

Learning to let go of my imaginary superlatives was a difficult task. Beginning to see my life for what it was after I started to regain my sanity was disheartening. I had to discover that there was no magic.

Sometimes I didn't know if I would ever completely let go of my fantasy life. It acted like a crutch sometimes when everything seemed lost. The disparity from my often-felt visionary past to my new and developing reality was a great divide. It felt like an impossible bridge to cross.

Realizing that I was mentally ill made me question what my capabilities were. My actual abilities were turning out to be less than I had previously believed. Some skills that I used in previous employment seemed to be of little use anymore. My past aspirations were beginning to appear unattainable.

I know there had always been sound and sane parts of my life, and they continued to exist. I discovered that I would need to fill in some gaps, though.

Appreciating the importance of having people in my life was rather new for me. Having supports and friends was something that I would have to work toward. Social skills had always been in need of improvement, and now that seemed to be truer than ever. I would need to find a new lifestyle that kept my illness in check, yet also had some enjoyment and purpose to it.

Self-doubt continued to plague me even as I grew stronger in new ways. Though I had given up old dreams of happiness and success, I set my goals so as to strive for new ones.

There were questions of my mind's ability to make rational decisions, which put limits on my expectations for a prosperous future. My thoughts had come to some unusual conclusions while I was so deeply troubled. They needed to be sorted out.

At first, as I began to accept my disability, I thought that maybe it was my new and primary characteristic that would forever define me. I knew I couldn't wish it away anymore.

After getting out of the hospital, my first doctor told me that I could live a normal and productive life. She said that though there was not a magic cure, the illness could be managed. In the beginning I couldn't get around the question of my new identity. "So this is my new life," I thought.

I wanted to know what role the illness had been playing in my life and how it would affect my future. I wanted to understand what it had done to me in the past. Where had it taken me? Where would it take me? Could I control it, or would it control me?

Finding perspective on my life and the role of my disability has been an undertaking. A stepping-stone in my early recovery was when I began to acknowledge that I was more than my illness. It took even longer to realize that I could build a life for myself, even though it might not include my prior dreams of professional achievement and financial success.

First I practiced writing, and then I learned to talk about the stillness and emptiness of my inner self. I began to learn that I was not such a stranger. I began to understand that my feelings were real, as my life had been. It was just unknown to almost anyone. My feelings had been cloaked for a long time.

I tried to get a realistic point of view. What kind of future could there be? I felt that I had lost so much opportunity. So much time had passed where I should have been growing along with my peers. My limited social contact seemed to have left me behind.

Breaking the barriers between the distorted mind and the real world was confusing. Finding meaning and making sense of the losses has stretched over years of therapy and introspection. Sometimes I just seemed to barely function, not gaining any understanding or true acceptance of why this illness became part of my life.

After my release from the hospital, I looked to memories

of my past. I needed to create a new life out of what seemed like nothing.

Remembering things that I used to do and trying them again was a start. I liked walking early in the morning when the air was still fresh. It was invigorating in the colder temperatures. In the spring and summer, lush smells were welcome to breathe in. Stars in the sky at night were exciting to gaze at. Noticing the phases of the moon was also an enjoyment. Immersing myself in the moment let me feel a little bit alive.

I liked walking to the coffee shop for a small black coffee and an occasional doughnut. I would often sit and read the paper in the morning and glance up at the people as they placed their orders at the counter.

I found landscaping to be a relatively low-stress line of work that kept my mind occupied. I found enjoyment being outdoors, as I often had in my past both before and during my sickness.

When I began to practice cooking and doing the shopping and the planning that goes along with the process, it became a new challenge and then an enjoyment. It helped build my self-esteem knowing that I could make a meal, however simple it may have been. It also gave me something to talk about. It was an interest that I could share.

Though I hoped and prayed to be made anew and quickly regain my strengths, I slowly learned that it was going to take time.

Time — and for me, a great deal of time — has been necessary to adjust to the changed outlook on life and its possible rewards. Dreams still existed, but they took on less aspiration of wealth and success after I began seeing life with more realistic eyes.

It became hard to imagine a fulfilled life, knowing that I was mentally ill. I worried at great length over what I would be able to do. How strong could I become? There was so much that I had never done or known.

Eventually, re-evaluating the real challenges of my life would become essential. Missing an identity that I could call my own and recognition of my true self was a daily test. I offered myself hope and occasional prayers that I would become well and that I would discover the life that had been hidden from me for so long.

Beginning to determine the differences between what I believed of myself in the past compared to what was true was a delicate act at first. It was like hovering on the brink of major depression. The task was too huge, I felt. To discover that in truth I was suffering a mental illness was life-shattering, when I first began to acknowledge it deep in my heart.

Conversely, there was also a great deal of relief to have an explanation for the endless grief that I had previously experienced for so many years. Now there was the offer of hope and wellness.

First I had to learn about my disorder, and then I had to undergo a process of becoming a new person. Gradually I began to manage my life a little better.

By learning and perceiving the nature of my long-term distress, I thought I would now have a chance to recover. I was told it was a process and it would take time.

Not until I had become hospitalized was I forced to surrender many opinions about myself. Certain beliefs were abruptly proven painfully untrue during and after my nine-month hospitalization. Being put in a psychiatric hospital stopped me in my tracks. I was devastated when my imaginary world was gone. It had been a useful resource to defend against my solitude.

There doesn't seem to be an explanation for the losses, other than life taking its own course. It simply happened, due to some apparent combination of genetic and environmental reasons. At this point in my life I haven't been able to find any satisfactory grand plan to explain all that has happened. I have found friends and understanding along the way, though.

It seems better to live in the day and find happiness there. I feel better when I'm less concerned with trying to comprehend my illness. The need to justify my life or to explain it has lessened. As far as finding value from the experience, I think growing and finding rewards in helping other people are good goals to live by today.

EPILOGUE

It's now twelve years since my release from the psychiatric hospital in 2000. Nine months of hospitalization had been spent reassessing my thoughts and wondering what lay ahead.

I first put pen to paper while still on the ward, as I attempted to settle my disheveled mind and plot out a new future for myself. I began to dream of a day when it would all make sense. Initially I wrote for my own benefit as something of a journal. This later helped me explain the inner workings of my mind to my family and my therapists.

Today I'm sharing my writing with a wider audience in the hope that some may benefit from my experience. By putting my story to paper, I'm fulfilling a dream. This is, in a large part, the book that I was looking to read when I was first released from the hospital. I desperately sought to be able to relate my thoughts and feelings with another person.

Sadly, it took me becoming arrested before I could fully accept my illness. I hope this part of my story doesn't add to the stigma of mental illness, but rather, that it may encourage others to seek help before it comes to that point.

My family remains very supportive. Also I am involved in a wonderful relationship with a woman I met at a NAMI (National Alliance on Mental Illness) support group meeting. She is a joy to be with, and has been inspirational in the completion this book. Friends are still few, but I know things can change.

Employment remains a challenge. Over the years I have worked mostly in landscaping and recently at a garden center. I had a few short-term office jobs but they never materialized into full time employment. Though I was offered a great job after a number of years into recovery, the stress and responsibilities were too much for me. I felt truly dejected after failing to capitalize on that opportunity. It's hard to find just the right employment that is rewarding yet not too stressful.

As long as I continue with my medications and see my therapist on a regular basis, I manage my symptoms well today. My delusional mind has all but subsided and the depression that once suppressed me has left. I occasionally recall the manic thrill, but today I respect the risks of an untreated illness and have no real desire to explore that realm again.

CPSIA information can be obtained at www.ICGtesting.com
Printed in the USA
LVOW11s1517050515

437311LV00001B/105/P